To
nana

FROM Mikaela & Thomas

THE GIFT ANGEL

G

THE GIFT ANGEL

AIRDRIE THOMSEN

SIMON AND SCHUSTER
New York · London

Published in the United States of America by
Simon and Schuster
A Division of Simon & Schuster, Inc.
Simon & Schuster Building
Rockefeller Center
1230 Avenue of the Americas
New York, New York 10020

Published in Great Britain by
Simon and Schuster Limited
A Division of Simon & Schuster, Inc.
West Garden Place, Kendal Street
London W2 2AQ

Designed by Airdrie Thomsen
Manufactured in Spain
Printed and bound by Novograph, S.A.

1   3   5   7   9   10   8   6   4   2

British Library Cataloguing-in-Publication Data

Thomsen, Airdrie Anne
The gift angel.
I. Title
813'.54 [J]   PZ7
ISBN 0-671-65466-7

Library of Congress Cataloging-in-Publication Data

Thomsen, Airdrie.
The gift angel.

1. English language—Alphabet—Juvenile literature.
2. Angels in art—Juvenile literature. [1. Angels—
Pictorial works. 2. Alphabet.] I. Title.
PE1155.T48   1987   [E]   87-9438
ISBN 0-671-64334-7

A ALPHABET
ANGEL

B

C
CASTLE AIGEL

D

ANGELS OF THE DANCE

ANGELS OF THE DANCE

E ELEPHANT ANGEL

F ANGELS FISHING

ANGEL OF THE GONDOLA

ANGEL OF THE GONDOLA

H ANGEL OF THE HILLSIDE

I · ANGEL IN LOVE

ANGEL
OF
JAMS & JELLIES

M ANGEL OF MIDSUMMER NIGHT

ANGEL
NESTING

OCEAN GOING ANGEL

P ANGELS PICNICKING

ANGELS PICNICKING

ANGEL QUEEN

ANGEL of ROSES

R

S

T ANGEL OF THE TREE-TOP

U UMBRELLAS ANGEL

V

ANGEL
VALENTINE

W

ANGEL OF THE WIND

ANGEL OF THE WIND

X XYLOPHONE ANGELS

Y our angel

Z ZOOMING ANGELS